SHINE!

inspirational poetry
with spoken word CD
by
Tonya Marie Evans

"Seasons" Cover Art by Bernard A. Collins, Jr.
Cover Photograph Copyright © 2000 by Steve Booth

Layout and Design by Stephanie Renée
for Creator's Child Productions, Inc.

To Darnley,
Thanks for your support and continue
to shine!

www.FYOS.com

FYOS Publishing,
a division of FYOS Entertainment, LLC
Philadelphia 2000
Second Printing
First Edition

www.fyos.com

FYOS Publishing,
a division of FYOS Entertainment, LLC

FYOS Publishing books may be purchased from your local bookstore or directly from the publisher. Please visit www.fyos.com.

Second Printing
First Edition
Designed by Creator's Child Productions, Inc.

ISBN# 0-9674579-3-9

First giving honor to my Creator,
I dedicate this work to my mother, father, family
and the FYOS family
for encouraging me to illuminate my own life path and the
paths of others
with the ever-present glow of creativity.

Table of Contents

Foreword

All aboard for SHINE!, the next stop on my poetic journey to encourage you to find your own shine. After many of my performances while on tour with my first book, Seasons of Her, many of you shared with me that hearing the voice of the poet who wrote the poems really allowed you to feel the emotion behind each word, each syllable, each sigh and each intonation. During the performances, you discovered that you received the words in person in a way that was distinctively different from the experience of reading the poetry with your own internal voice. You reported that both experiences — reading and hearing the words — gave you something unique and equally enjoyable. You found that you could not choose one medium over the other. You wanted both! It seemed that you reveled in the written word and the ability to linger over the lines, and at the same time you longed for the poet's voice to complete the sensory circle. Thus, SHINE! was born, the perfect blend of the written and spoken word.

SHINE! is the blessed response to your requests for a book of poetry AND spoken word CD. What better way to share my Self with you than to share my words, my voice and my essence all in one dynamic package. But I did not stop at merely recording live performances of the words. I combined the poems with a soulful blend of neosoul and funk inspired musical tracks to make your head bob to the beat and reflect on the message simultaneously!

I hope and trust that through this multimedia book you will tap into that essential spark of greatness within you. The CD contained in SHINE! will be the music you will listen to in those quiet, reflective moments AND the music you blaze when you are pushin' your jeep on the highway! So ease into your greatness and get ready to SHINE!

SHINE!

inspirational poetry

"You are like light for the whole world. A city built on a hill cannot be hid. No one lights a lamp and puts it under a bowl; instead he [or she] puts it on the lampstand, where it gives light for everyone in the house. In the same way your light must shine before people, so that they will see the good things you do and praise your Father in Heaven." Matt. 5:14 -16

Today's English Version, Second Edition © 1992

Journey
1991

Blessed with the ultimate gift
LIFE
I struggle and fight to fulfill my
DREAMS
Before my few precious moments on this
EARTH
Become as untouchable, as incomprehensible as
WIND

I Will Tell Myself
1997

No one will tell me what it is I can be.
No one will determine my self worth
or define me but me.
Try if you will but you will be committing
an act against God
because it's a sin
to waste valuable energy.

The Creator planted in me
embers of greatness that I must ignite,
that I must enrage into a torrent of fire
to consume self-doubt and self-hate.
So I have no time to wait
for others to recognize ...
because a bird that has wings
needs no one to tell it when to fly.

The responsibility is great
and I have no time to waste
on pre-packaged constructions of my
SUPPOSED WORTHLESSNESS
especially my supposed sexual prowess
— The Venus Hottentot I am not —
I Sojourn on a path of Truth
not lies and alibis created to confuse.

— I am not confused —
I am convinced that
I have greatness within
and I am a Superwoman
able to leap
TALL DECEPTION
in a single bound.

Self image, by definition, cannot depend
on the beliefs of others.
So stop looking to others to decide
who you are ... what you are ...
what you should say or do.
Only you should tell you.
And if you choose not to
the vulnerability you will face
cannot be measured.
But as for me,
I will tell myself.

And no Supreme Court decision
will keep me from my education,
no legislation will keep me
from feeding my kids,
no book of rules will tell me
how to satisfy my man,
no church will tell me to be seen
and not heard.

Nobody is gonna tell me nothing!

Because my ears are keenly attuned
to the sweet serenade of GREATNESS
sung amidst chariots that swing low,
in the jails of Birmingham,
in front of hoses and dogs,
on elementary school steps,
in churches that burn,
in cotton fields and on kitchen floors,
on the bottoms of ships,
in rich African nations,

and yes ...
within my own intimate temple
right here, right now
so I will tell myself ...
and everyone else will listen!

Wild Child
1995

Hanging too loose and running too wild,
you are a wild child on the run.
But your legs are spread too wide to run freely.
So, with head down and braced against reason
you dart and weave through on-coming traffic
either oblivious or unconcerned
with the head-on collision in your reckless path.
Instead of allowing wisdom to illuminate your way
you prefer to blindly nose out danger in every race.
You throw up your hand, suck your teeth
and continue to sex with no expression ...
no protection
having no time to waste on connecting or reflecting
and the concept of conception not even considered
because you figure
"can't happen to me ... again."

You have two that went to term, others terminated
and your mom is frustrated cause
she suckles the grands while
her child runs wild.
But you have no time for your mom's tears
cause you have to keep running to that
next bump ... that next grind ...
that next time you seek the love you desire
in thick, sweaty arms and hot quick breaths.

Till that next chance you take
as you beg countless mouths
to whisper all those vacant words ...
the ones you've already heard, but never believed.

In response to the lies, you grab hold, holding tight
as you near the moment when you hope to receive
the feeling you're seeking.
But when he stands to pull up his pants
over the shoes he still wears
you turn away with salty drops burning your face
and this is the one time when you are still ...
and I know for sure you despise how that feels.
Because while his sex is draining from your thighs,
you realize the love you sought
drains away too.

Like the addict who hits the wall, inevitably
you free fall
and kick your legs frantically
in an attempt to regain your speed.
You keep moving
keep running
keep running
keep running
while love continues to be blurred
by the dizzy pace you maintain.

All along people wonder why you just don't stop.
But I already know why ...
it's 'cause you're hanging too loose
and running too wild,

you are a wild child on the run.

A Villager Speaks

1995

The ancestors have said
that it takes a village to raise you, my child
and I am only one of many who will influence you,
but I want to do my part to help shape and mold you
so you, still a child, will be stronger than I
by the time you reach your prime.

Now I may get close to the you
nobody knew but you
that time you ran away,
but this time I hope you'll stay
and listen to what this villager has to say.
I know you think the experiences of my day
can't compare and you'd rather
do things your way.
Believe me, your point is well made,
for your lethal crack pipes
far outweigh my Mary Jane daze.

And the fact that you've stood
in the halls of abandoned buildings
surrounded by filth, broken glass
and the stench of last week's killings
means your soul has indeed grown old.
But your addict ways lead you astray ...
away from the proper way a child should grow.

Now, your real age far outweighs
the chronological order of days
you've stood on this planet
BUT DAMMIT ...
you've got to slow down.

In your formative days
while other village youth waited,
you shot out of the blocks with reckless speed.
The problem is you didn't wait
for the blast of the starter's gun
to signal that it was time for you to run.
Didn't you realize that false starts mean
you never reach the finish line?

Somehow your spirit became disconnected
from the life force of the village,
the flow that flows through each villager
and connects each to the other.
And your disconnected spirit
sought reconnection in a dangerous place ...
where broken spirits congregate
to receive their holy hits.
With body drawn and weak,
mind weaker,
and ears deafened to the medicinal hum
of ancestral voices
you may think you are forever lost
with no way to find your way home ...
back to the safety of the village.

But don't worry, child …
you are still young
and until you take your last breath,
you will always have time
to return to your place of origin
and begin again.

Did you hear me, child?

Until you take your last breath,
you will always have time
to return to your place of origin
and begin again …

Listen, child,
return to your place of origin
and begin again.

I Know You
1995
for Ayanna

Ever since I heard you read that poem
when you spoke the name
of the guy who stole your soul,
the one who raped you
and shattered your fragility,
I have wanted to reach out to you.
I wanted to
grab you,
hug you,
cry in your embrace
and tell you that
I know you.

I know you because
that hell you believed left you alone,
it's not just your own.
That claustrophobic space
you feel trapped in
whenever some sister reveals her
smoldering rage of pain,
I am cramped in there too.
It's dark, so maybe you can't see me,
but I am there ...
I am there with you.

That night you spoke his name
and my claustrophobia kicked in,
I tried to call out to you ...
I tried to fill my collapsed lungs
and scream,
"I KNOW YOU!"
But all I could muster was
a silent whisper that cried,
"here I am ... over here."
I hoped desperately
that you would hear me,
find me,
and join me
so we could draw strength
from our shared experience.
But on that night,
the night you spoke the name
of the guy who stole your soul,
I found I could not move
because my feet were frozen ...

      frozen like my body was
      when that alien invaded my space.

I froze because I suddenly remembered
forgotten memories
I had yet to forget.
And I got scared because those
forget-me-nevers
were still married to powerlessness.

But listening to you, I knew
if I could say the name
of the bastard who raped me,
then I could feel the power
you must feel every time you
flex your vocal chords
and seize public moments
to exorcise private demons.
I hope you know that when you speak
of your shattered fragility,
you speak for those
who have yet to find their voice ...
those like me
still muted by unspoken cries.

But your bravery returned sensation
to my paralyzed limbs
and I reached out to bring to my lips
what was always there,
what was always mine ...
my truth,
—The Truth —
the one thing I needed
to damn his flood of lies.

The Truth is that, although
I screamed many things that afternoon,
"RAPE ME"
was not one of them.
The Truth is that it is indeed possible
to be raped by the man
you call your man.

The Truth is that
when I was violated
by the man I called my man,
my reality was crucified
because I only expected such atrocities
from strangers.

The Truth is that
Greg,
the man who was my man,
who raped me,
was a stranger.
A stranger with
strange eyes,
strange hands,
strange sounds,
strange words,
strange intentions.

The Truth is that,
Sister,
I know you.
And I can finally let my guard down
and tell you so
because you have
shown me how
powerful
vulnerability can be.
Not a weakness, but a supreme form of
honesty
which I will use
to bond my shattered pieces
and regain wholeness.

Angry Don't Live Here No More
1995

Shhhhh …
Lower your voice.
Angry don't live here no more
and Peace, He don't care for all that drama.
All that yellin', cussin' and spittin' you flippin' is old.
Thought somebody told you, Angry's gone.

Naw, sorry, Fear was peaced too.
Angry grabbed her up, wrapped her tight
and broke out when Peace came around.
Doubt and Jealousy used to hang out
from time to time
but things just ain't the same
now that Angry's gone …
Don't attract the same crowd.

Used to be all funky and musty
from all the folks up in here
but now the air is mellow and sweet,
cause Peace burns that incense
when He's on His knees.
He don't even have light bulb the first.
Says He don't need one cause He is light …

Now I don't have any idea what all that means,
but the Brothuh does seem to glow.
In fact, right after Angry snuck out the back
a smile came to Peace's face
that damn near blinded me.

Tripped me out!
And scared Gloom right outta here.
Huh, never seen Gloom move so fast.

Sometimes I feel bad for Peace though ...
Doesn't keep as much company as Angry did.
Now when Angry was here, the place was packed.
Wall to wall folks hangin' all out
the doors and the windows.
People like
Depression and Violence
Death and Destruction
Paranoia, Pissed and Foul.
All the folks was up in here.
Even Denial would put his thing down.

But Peace, He just has a few people he hangs with:
Now, Love is always here,
Serenity, she comes through.
And Happiness ... can't get that Brothuh outta here!
I see Hope all the time
cause that's Peace's sistuh, ya know.

Yeah, the place sure has changed
now that Angry's gone.
Now when Angry was here,
I couldn't hear myself think.
All that poundin' and screamin' over my head
it just took over my mind.
I was always on edge cause I could never tell
what was gonna happen next.

But since Peace moved in
all I can hear is myself thinking ...
In fact, if I wasn't talkin' right now
wouldn't hear nothin',
'cept maybe my breathin' or my blood pumpin'.

Come to think of it,
I still don't know what to expect upstairs.
But now it don't much matter,
now that Peace lives here, ya know?

That Bitch of Life
1995

There have been those times in my life
when I have been unsure of myself.
Times when I displayed an awkward gait
and I felt I needed some defining measure
to show the world I had myself together,
cause I didn't want anyone to
perceive my weaknesses.
So I'd jump up and down
and scream at the top of my lungs,
to create a physical diversion.
And when all eyes were fixed on me,
my legs were so filled with confidence
that the soles of my feet
contradicted the mandates of gravity.
With attention pointed in my direction,
I felt I could leap to dream-filled heights,
stretch and contort with all my might,
believing all possibilities were within my sight ...
And I wore a smile that said,
"I have myself together!"

It was times like those when I believed
whoever said life is a bitch
was a damned fool.
I thought they just didn't know how to roll,
didn't know how to take control.

Too busy crying and denying to know what I know.
Cause I was told
if I devised a plan, ran it to the letter,
and others respected me,
I'd have myself together.

Did it in school … 4.0 showed I wasn't a fool.
Did it in sport … proved brown folk
could do work on a tennis court.
I rode that fragile false confidence for a while,
until that Bitch of life I'd heard about
jumped all in my smiling face,
snarling and baring her teeth
like the rabid dog that she is.
She took me all out of my groove, and
that confident flow … flew.
She rearranged everything I thought I knew,
made me recoil and I withdrew.
I went into myself in order to seek the comfortable place
that Bitch of life tried to erase.

And when I was inside of me,
I tried to make sense of what had gone wrong with my
plan.
Tried to understand how I could close my eyes one night
and awaken bewildered by all that once seemed familiar.
I took myself into my arms, held me tight,
stroked my hair and dried my eyes.
And when I was quiet and ever so still …
what I was seeking suddenly appeared within my sights.

I found out the hard way that there wasn't any
cure-all in those judgmental eyes
to silence my internal confusion.
But more than that, I found out
I didn't know all I thought
cause in reality ...
that Bitch of life
was me.
The me I denied when I tried
to prove myself to the outside.

Now when I walk, I still glide,
I still have a confident stride ...
but the purpose of walking tall
is simply to hold my head high.
I don't waste any time waiting for others to see me
cause I see me and I like what I see!
And if you do too ... that's cool.
If not ... that's on you.
I'm no longer wasting time trying to find my perfection
in others' eyes ...
I'm too busy looking
inside
for when that Bitch of life rolls up again.

And she will ... I know she will.

She's lurking somewhere nearby
waiting for any sign
of that awkward gait...

But now that I know myself
it's gonna be a long wait.

Black Child
1991

You,
Black Child,
are a mover, a shaker
of African descent,
the original royalty.

Hold Your head high
and let the glow
of the sun
brighten the future
in Your eyes.

Feel the strength
of Your spirit
as it stirs within
Your newly formed bones
and solidifies
Your impressionable flesh.

A plethora of possibilities
await Your arrival.
Therefore, balk at those
who prophesize the end,
for it is only a myth
as long as You exist,
Black Child.

Find Your Own Shine
1997

Gracefully,
I elude spiritual land mines
of doubt, jealousy and envy
deceitfully planted by those
who despise divine DIVAS like me.
Those who waste valuable energy
wondering
who I be,
how I be,
why I be so fly?
How it is I can laugh and sing
and hold my head high
while it rains and thunders all around me

and never get wet?

But their confusion
is confusing to me
cause I see the answer so clearly ...
I am a child of God,
a unique and individual gift
to this universe,
an angel, who understands
from whence my blessings flow,
an appreciator of the expansiveness
of my earth-toned wings.

And
I feel my own rays of sun shining
I feel my melodies of life singing
I feel my righteous rivers raging
I feel my defiant winds swirling

I feel my flowers growing
I feel my beauty showing!

Consistently exuding stealth
like the sleekest jaguar,
cause I've come to understand
it's truly hard being a star.
People constantly looking up at my shine
wishing all the time it wasn't really mine.

But it is God given, and I've claimed it
and now I own it,
and I would lay in an unmarked grave
before I allow greedy hands to steal my joy.

Lord knows it ain't easy
but no one promised it would be
and now I see why.
I must be forever dynamic,
in constant motion
as lightness and levity
elevate me toward a sky of positivity,
in order to avoid those
who spend time wishing they weren't
blinded by my shine.

See, they whine
and weight themselves down.
Guess that woulda-coulda-shoulda stuff
be too heavy to carry around.

Maybe that explains why they be plagued
by permanent frowns.
Constant melancholy state,
awkward gait,
that hurry-up-and-wait
to see if maybe this will be the day
when this DIVA falls from grace.
From my rightful place in the sky.
Calling my self-affirmations
ego trippin' or conceit …

They just can't feel me like I feel me,
like my Creator feels me,

Like I feel me!

But still they observe me
and wonder how they can capture my glow,
while I long for the day when they discover
they already have their own.

Find your own shine.

Acknowledgements

First, I give honor to the Creator! I would like to thank my mother/partner/mentor/sister/friend Susan Borden Evans, Esq., for joining me in this exciting literary endeavor that is FYOS Entertainment, LLC. We planted the seed only one year ago. Since that time, our baby seedling has blossomed and continues to flourish beyond our wildest imaginings. Your loving and compassionate support and belief in me has allowed me to shine in every aspect of life. Thank you!

I would also like to thank my father, Dr. Richard Allan Evans, who constantly and consistently encourages me to be better than the best and to "never let 'em see you sweat." And thanks for passing on the poetic genes, Dude!

To the rest of my family, especially my Nana, thank you for loving me and encouraging me every step of the way. To Brittany (a/k/a Bricks) and John Jr. (a/k/a Peeps), keep that creative spark alive and nourish it day and night!

To my sister/poet/friend, Stephanie Renée McNeal, thank you for giving your all to this project at every level of production! We're on our way, Diva … see you at the top!

Thanks to Damon "Mr. Dizzy Fingers" Bennett for loving this project "like a play cousin" and putting your 'thang' down to take SHINE! to the next level of professionalism and creativity. The beats, music and flute solo are slammin'!

I would also like to thank my friends, especially the Ivy Investments crew, for their continued support and for keeping me grounded in this time of cataclysmic change in my life.

Lastly, thanks to the many exceptionally talented poets and writers who continue to encourage me along the way, especially Monica Blache, Franklin White and Kathleen Cross. Please remember to support Black authors, book booksellers and literary communities (like the African American Online Writers Guild (aaowg.org))!

About The Author

Tonya Marie Evans, Esq., author of Seasons of Her, is also known as the "Lawyer by Day, Poet by Night." She is a Dean's List graduate of Northwestern University and former student-athlete who received a full four-year tennis scholarship (87-91). Tonya Marie also competed on the professional women's tennis tour for four years before giving up the tennis court for the court of law. Her most notable competitions include the Virginia Slims of Philadelphia, the Lipton and the US Open.

Tonya Marie is also a cum laude graduate of Howard University School of Law (HUSL). At HUSL, Tonya Marie was Editor-In-Chief of the Howard Law Journal. She has since published a law review article, entitled *The Intersectionality of Race and Gender in the Context of Intercollegiate Athletics*. During the day, she practices law in the areas of estate planning and entertainment. At night she melts mics with her poetic reveries.

Tonya Marie currently resides in Philadelphia and is a member of Alpha Kappa Alpha Sorority, Inc.

www.fyos.com

About FYOS℠

Tonya Marie Evans, Esq. and Susan Borden Evans, Esq., the founders of FYOS℠ Entertainment, LLC, are a mother/daughter team of vision and purpose. FYOS℠ is dedicated to the Kwanzaa concept of Kujichagulia (Self-Determination) in art and in business pursuits. They have chosen to maintain control over their publications and performances — not as a last resort — but as the first choice!

They represent the perfect union of artist, agent and family. One is an artist; both are attorneys. They boast that they represent themselves, write for themselves and provide a loving and nurturing environment for themselves and other authors of African descent. They are committed to producing publications and live performances that intrigue, inspire, motivate, encourage, and challenge connoisseurs of the spoken and written word.

FYOS℠ publications are sold directly on the Internet at www.fyos.com, Cushcity.com and Amazon.com. FYOS℠ titles are also distributed nationally and are available at your local bookstore.

Books published by FYOS^{SM} Publishing:

Seasons of Her: a collection of poetry
by Tonya Marie Evans
ISBN 0-9674579-0-4
$15.00 (paperback)
(Pub. 1999)

SHINE! inspirational poetry (w/ spoken word CD)
by Tonya Marie Evans
ISBN 0-9674579-3-9
$16.00 (paperback)
(Pub. 2000)

An Old Soul Reborn (Poetry)
by Tonya Marie Evans
ISBN 0-9674579-2-0
$15.00 (paperback)
(Pub. 2001)

The Blues (Fiction)
by Tonya Marie Evans
ISBN 0-9674579-1-2
$22.00 (hardback)
(Pub. 2001)

To order any FYOS^{SM} publication directly from the publisher,
send the proper payment and $3.55 S&H per copy to
FYOS Entertainment, LLC, P.O. Box 2021, Phila., PA 19103
or visit www.fyos.com to place your credit card order.

Special pricing options for booksellers, wholesalers, libraries,
and for book clubs that order 10 or more copies of any title,
directly from the publisher.

SHINE!
The Companion CD

1. Introduction: Whuhbump

2. I Will Tell Myself

3. Angry Don't Live Here No More*+

4. A Villager Speaks**

5. Black Child

6. Find Your Own Shine*

All Lyrics written by Tonya Marie Evans (ASCAP)
Lead and Background Vocals by Tonya Marie Evans
* Background Vocals by Stephanie Renée (ASCAP)
+ Additional Vocals by L.I.F.E.
** Flute Solo by Damon "Mr. Dizzy Fingers" Bennett

Produced by Damon Bennett
Executive Producers: Tonya Marie Evans and Stephanie Renée
(Creator's Child Productions, Inc.)
Mastered and Manufactured by DiscMakers